AI For Grannies

A Friendly Guide to AI for the Elderly

(And Not So...)

Book 1

A Series of 10 Books to Learn Together

PUBLISHED BY: Sergio Prizont

Sergio Prizont

Table of Contents

Introduction: AI Is Not Just for Tech People, It's for You Too!

You've probably heard people talking about **Artificial Intelligence (AI),** maybe on the news, in conversations, or even from your grandkids. Maybe someone said, "AI is the future!" and you thought, *That sounds complicated... and not for me.*

But here's the truth: **AI is not just for tech people. AI is for everyone, including you.**

In fact, **you're probably already using AI** without realizing it. Ever asked Siri or Alexa a question? That's AI. Used Google Maps to find the fastest route? AI did that for you. Got a product recommendation while shopping online? AI again.

So, no, AI is **not just robots taking over the world.** It's a tool, one that can **make life easier, help with everyday tasks, and even be fun.** And the best part? You **don't** need to be a computer expert to use it.

Why This Book?

This book is for people who **don't know anything about AI** but are **curious to learn.** If you're here, it means you want to understand what AI is and how you can use it in real life. And I promise, you won't find any **confusing tech jargon** or boring explanations here.

Instead, you'll get:

Simple, clear explanations, no complicated words, just real talk.

Fun and useful ways to try AI yourself.
Step-by-step guidance, so you never feel lost.
Two hands-on exercises at the end, so you can **practice using AI right away.**

What You'll Learn

By the end of this book, you'll be able to:

- **Understand what AI is (and what it isn't).**

- **Talk to AI and get useful answers.**

- **Use AI to help with daily life, like reminders, writing, and learning new things.**

- **Try out AI tools that are simple and free.**

- **Know how to ask AI better questions to get better answers.**

And most importantly, you'll feel **confident using AI instead of intimidated by it.**

What This Book Is NOT

Before we dive in, let's clear something up. This book is **not** going to teach you how to **build AI or write computer code.** You don't need that. AI is already made, **you just need to learn how to use it.**

Think of it like a car. You don't need to build an engine to drive, you just need to learn **how to turn the key and hit the gas.**

AI is the same way. You don't have to be a tech genius to use it. **You just need to know how to ask the right questions.**

How to Read This Book

Each chapter will walk you through a new piece of AI, from **what it is** to **how you can use it right now.** You'll find:

Real-life examples (so AI feels useful, not scary). **Step-by-step instructions** (so you can follow along easily). **Practical exercises** at the end (so you can test what you've learned).

And don't worry, **you can take your time.** AI isn't going anywhere, so go at your own pace and enjoy the learning process!

Let's Get Started!

By the time you finish this book, AI will feel **less like a mystery and more like a helpful tool you can actually use.**

So, are you ready to take your first step into the world of AI? Let's get started!

CHAPTER 1: What is AI, and Why Should You Care?

Understanding AI in the Simplest Way Possible

AI Is Not a Robot (Well, Not Always...)

If you hear the words "artificial intelligence" or "AI," what's the first thing that comes to mind? Maybe it's a talking robot from a science-fiction movie, like R2-D2 from *Star Wars* or the scary robots from *The Terminator*. Or maybe you think of something futuristic and complicated that only young people or scientists understand.

Well, here's the good news: AI is not a robot (at least, not always), and it's not as complicated as you might think. In fact, you're probably already using AI in your daily life without even realizing it! Let's break it down into the simplest terms so you can see what AI really is and how it can make your life easier.

AI Is Just a Fancy Name for "Smart Technology"

At its core, artificial intelligence is just smart technology that helps computers and devices learn and solve problems on their own. Instead of needing a person to tell them exactly what to do every single time, AI can figure things out based on patterns and past experiences.

Think about a regular calculator. If you type in 2 + 2, it will always tell you the answer is 4. But the calculator doesn't "learn" anything, it just follows instructions. Now, imagine a smartphone keyboard that learns the words you use most often and starts suggesting them for you. That's AI at work! It's learning and adapting to make things easier for you.

In other words, AI isn't magic, it's just a way for computers and devices to act a little smarter so they can help you more efficiently.

AI is Everywhere (And You've Probably Used It!)

Many people think AI is something futuristic, but the truth is, you're already surrounded by it. You might have even used it today! Here are some everyday examples:

- **Voice Assistants:** If you've ever asked Siri, Alexa, or Google Assistant a question, you've used AI. These smart helpers listen to your voice, understand what you're saying, and find answers for you.

- **Smartphone Keyboards:** When your phone suggests words while you're typing a message, that's AI predicting what you might say next.

- **TV and Movie Recommendations:** Ever noticed how Netflix or YouTube suggests shows you might like? That's AI learning your preferences and helping you find entertainment you enjoy.

- **Spam Filters in Email:** AI helps block spam emails so that junk mail doesn't clutter your inbox.

- **GPS and Traffic Apps:** AI helps navigation apps like Google Maps find the best route by checking live traffic conditions and adjusting directions as needed.

- **Online Shopping Suggestions:** If Amazon or another store recommends products based on what you've looked at before, that's AI helping you shop smarter.

See? AI is already part of your life, and you didn't even have to learn anything complicated to use it!

If AI Isn't a Robot, Then What Is It?

Many people associate AI with robots because that's what we see in movies. But AI is actually software, not hardware. That means AI is more like a "brain" that helps computers and devices think and learn, rather than a physical robot walking around.

Sure, there are AI-powered robots in factories, hospitals, and even homes (like robot vacuum cleaners), but most AI doesn't have a body at all. It's inside your phone, your computer, or even behind the scenes when you use the internet.

To put it simply:

- **A robot is a machine that moves and does physical tasks.**

- **AI is the smart technology that helps machines, computers, and programs think and learn.**

- **Sometimes, AI is inside a robot, but most of the time, it's just software working quietly in the background.**

AI is Like a Helpful Assistant (But It's Not Perfect!)

Think of AI as a helpful assistant that is always learning, but it's not perfect. Just like a new employee might make mistakes

Sergio Prizont

before they fully understand their job, AI can sometimes misunderstand things or give weird answers.

For example, have you ever tried talking to a voice assistant like Siri or Alexa and gotten a completely wrong answer? Maybe you asked, "What's the weather tomorrow?" and it replied, "Playing your favorite song." That's because AI is still learning, and it sometimes gets confused. But the more people use AI, the smarter it gets over time.

The important thing to remember is that AI is a tool. It's here to help, but it doesn't have feelings, opinions, or human understanding. It's good at solving problems, but it's not as smart as a real person.

Why Should You Care About AI?

Now that you know AI isn't just about robots, why should you care about it? Because AI is designed to make life easier, and once you understand how to use it, you can take advantage of its benefits!

Here are a few ways AI can help you:

- **Save Time:** AI can help you write emails faster, remind you about appointments, and even create shopping lists.

- **Stay Connected:** AI can translate languages so you can talk to family members who speak a different language.

- **Get Entertained:** AI helps recommend TV shows, movies, music, and even books based on what you like.

- **Stay Informed:** AI can summarize the news, give you weather updates, and even answer questions about history, health, or hobbies.

- **Improve Daily Tasks:** AI-powered smart home devices can adjust the temperature, turn on lights, or even lock your doors with a voice command.

AI isn't something to fear, it's something to use! And the best part? You don't have to be a tech expert to take advantage of AI. You just need to know what's possible and how to ask for help when you need it.

Final Thoughts

AI is not a scary, complicated robot from the movies. It's simply smart technology that helps make life easier. Whether it's helping you type messages, find the best driving route, or recommend a new TV show, AI is working behind the scenes to assist you every day.

The key takeaway? AI is not something far off in the future, it's here, now, and it's already helping you in ways you may not have even realized. And as you continue reading this book, you'll learn even more fun and simple ways AI can make your life better!

So, don't worry, you don't need a degree in computers to use AI. All you need is a little curiosity and a willingness to try new things. Who knows? You might even start enjoying AI as much as you enjoy a good cup of coffee or a chat with an old friend!

The Many Faces of AI

Artificial intelligence isn't just one thing, it shows up in many forms, each designed to help in a different way. AI can be on your phone, in your home, or even in your car. Some AI assistants talk to you, while others quietly work in the background to make your life easier. Let's take a closer look at the many faces of AI and how they show up in everyday life.

Voice Assistants vs. Chatbots: What's the Difference?

One of the most common ways people interact with AI is through voice assistants and chatbots. While they may seem similar, they are actually designed for different tasks.

Voice Assistants (Like Siri and Alexa)

Voice assistants are AI-powered programs that you can talk to. They recognize your voice and respond out loud. You've probably heard of Siri (on iPhones), Alexa (on Amazon Echo), or Google Assistant (on Android devices). These assistants are great for quick tasks like:

- Setting alarms and reminders

- Answering basic questions like "What's the weather today?"

- Playing music or audiobooks

- Controlling smart home devices (like lights and thermostats)

You simply ask them something out loud, and they give you an answer. However, voice assistants are not very "smart" when it comes to holding long conversations. They mostly follow commands and provide short answers.

Chatbots (Like ChatGPT and Customer Service Bots)

Chatbots are different. Instead of speaking out loud, you type your question, and the AI responds in text form. Chatbots are often found on websites, answering customer service questions. Some of the more advanced chatbots, like ChatGPT, can:

- Have detailed conversations

- Help with writing emails or documents

- Explain things in a simple way

- Even tell jokes or create stories

Unlike voice assistants, chatbots can carry on longer discussions and understand more complex requests. They are used for everything from customer support to helping students with homework.

Which One is Better? It depends on what you need! If you want quick, spoken answers, a voice assistant is best. If you need more detailed help, like writing an email or learning about a new topic, a chatbot might be the better choice.

AI in Phones, TVs, and Even Your Car

AI isn't just in assistants like Siri and Alexa, it's also built into many of the devices you use every day. Here's how AI is working behind the scenes to make life easier.

AI in Your Phone

Most modern smartphones have AI features that you might not even notice. Some examples include:

- **Autocorrect and Predictive Text:** When you type a message, your phone suggests words based on what you usually say. That's AI learning your writing style!

- **Face Recognition:** If you unlock your phone by looking at it, AI is scanning your face and matching it to your stored image.

- **Photo Organization:** AI sorts your photos into categories, recognizes faces, and even suggests the best pictures to keep.

AI in Your TV

Televisions have come a long way from just displaying channels. Many smart TVs use AI to:

- **Recommend Shows and Movies:** Platforms like Netflix and YouTube suggest content based on what you've watched before.

- **Improve Picture Quality:** Some TVs adjust brightness and contrast automatically depending on the room's lighting.

- **Understand Voice Commands:** Many TVs now have built-in voice assistants that let you search for shows just by talking.

AI in Your Car

Even your car may have AI built in! Many modern vehicles use AI to:

- **Provide GPS Directions:** AI-powered navigation apps help find the fastest routes by checking real-time traffic.

- **Assist with Parking:** Some cars can park themselves using AI-powered sensors and cameras.

- **Enhance Safety:** AI can detect when a driver is getting tired and suggest taking a break, or even apply emergency brakes if it senses danger.

As AI becomes more advanced, we may even see self-driving cars that can take us anywhere without human drivers!

The Different Types of AI (Without the Complicated Explanations)

Not all AI is the same. There are different types, each with a unique role. Let's break it down into simple terms.

1. Reactive AI (The Simple AI)

This is the most basic form of AI. It follows specific instructions and doesn't "learn" from past experiences. Examples include:

- A chess computer that follows set moves

- A spam filter that blocks junk emails based on pre-programmed rules

Reactive AI is useful, but it can't improve over time, it just does what it's told.

2. Limited Memory AI (The AI That Learns a Little)

This type of AI can remember past data for a short time and make better decisions based on that memory. Examples include:

- GPS apps that adjust routes based on real-time traffic updates

- Smart thermostats that learn your preferred temperature

Limited Memory AI is a step up because it adapts to what's happening right now.

3. AI with Understanding (The AI That "Thinks")

This AI is more advanced and can actually understand patterns and predict what might happen next. Some examples include:

- AI doctors that analyze medical scans to detect diseases early

- Chatbots like ChatGPT that can have meaningful conversations

This kind of AI is getting smarter over time, helping in areas like healthcare, finance, and even education.

4. Self-Aware AI (The AI of the Future)

Right now, AI does not have emotions or self-awareness. But in the distant future, scientists believe AI could develop a more human-like understanding of the world. For now, though, AI is just a smart tool, it doesn't have feelings or opinions.

Why Does This Matter to You?

Now that you know about the many faces of AI, you might be wondering: why should you care?

Well, understanding AI helps you make better choices. If you know how AI works:

- You can use it to make life easier (like using voice assistants to set reminders or GPS apps to find the fastest route).

- You can be aware of what AI is doing in the background (like recognizing how Netflix suggests shows for you).

- You won't be intimidated by new technology because now, you understand it!

AI is not something to fear; it's something to use. And the more you learn about it, the more you'll see how it's quietly making everyday tasks simpler, faster, and even more fun.

Final Thoughts

AI is not just one thing, it has many faces. From the voice assistant in your phone to the GPS in your car, AI is helping in ways you might not even notice. Some AI follows simple commands, while others learn and adapt to help even more.

The best part? You don't have to be a tech expert to take advantage of AI. It's already built into the devices you use every day. Now that you know how AI works in different forms, you can start using it to make life easier, whether it's asking Alexa for a weather update, getting Netflix to recommend your next favorite show, or using GPS to find the best route home.

So the next time someone mentions AI, you can smile and say, "I know all about that!" Because now, you do.

AI Is Here to Help (Not Take Over)

AI might sound like something out of a science fiction movie, but in reality, it's here to make life easier, not to replace people. From improving healthcare to making daily tasks more convenient, AI is helping in ways you might not have even realized. So, let's take a closer look at how AI is working for good, why it can't replace humans, and why now is the perfect time to learn about it (no matter how old you are!).

How AI is Used for Good: Healthcare, Accessibility, Safety

While AI is often associated with things like voice assistants or smart TVs, it is also being used in much bigger ways to improve lives. Here are some of the most impactful areas where AI is making a real difference.

AI in Healthcare: Helping Doctors and Patients

AI is changing the way healthcare works, helping doctors diagnose diseases faster and more accurately. In the past, finding signs of illnesses like cancer or heart disease in medical scans took a lot of time. Now, AI can analyze thousands of scans in minutes, helping doctors detect problems earlier and start treatment sooner.

Some examples of AI in healthcare include:

- **Detecting Diseases Early:** AI programs can examine X-rays, MRIs, and other medical scans to spot warning signs of illnesses, sometimes even before symptoms appear.

- **Helping Doctors with Diagnoses:** AI-powered tools can compare a patient's symptoms with medical databases to suggest possible conditions.

- **Assisting with Elderly Care:** AI can remind people to take their medications, monitor heart rates, and even alert caregivers if something seems off.

AI is not replacing doctors, it's simply giving them better tools to make informed decisions and provide better care.

AI for Accessibility: Making Life Easier for Everyone

AI is also helping people with disabilities lead more independent lives. Some examples include:

- **Speech-to-Text Technology:** AI-powered apps can transcribe spoken words into text for people who are deaf or hard of hearing.

- **Screen Readers:** These AI-driven tools can read out loud what's on a screen for people who have vision impairments.

- **Smart Assistants:** AI-powered assistants like Alexa and Google Assistant help people control lights, adjust the thermostat, or even make phone calls using just their voice.

For many, AI is not just a convenience, it's a game-changer that makes daily life more accessible.

AI in Safety: Preventing Accidents and Protecting People

AI is also making the world safer in ways that many people don't notice. Some examples include:

- **Self-Driving Car Safety Features:** AI helps cars detect obstacles, automatically brake if a collision is about to happen, and even alert drivers if they seem too tired to drive.

- **Fraud Detection in Banking:** AI keeps an eye on financial transactions and can spot unusual activity, like someone using your credit card number in another country, and block fraudulent charges before they happen.

- **Emergency Alerts and Disaster Response:** AI can predict natural disasters, like hurricanes or earthquakes, by analyzing patterns in weather data, helping people prepare in advance.

These are just a few of the many ways AI is being used to keep people safe and improve the world around us.

Can AI Replace Humans? (Spoiler: Not Really.)

One of the biggest fears people have about AI is that it will take over human jobs. But the truth is, AI is not here to replace people, it's here to assist them.

While AI can process data quickly and follow instructions, it lacks something very important: human creativity, emotions, and judgment.

What AI Can Do Well

AI is great at tasks that require:

- **Speed:** AI can process huge amounts of information in seconds, much faster than any person.

- **Repetition:** AI never gets bored or tired, making it perfect for jobs that involve repetitive tasks, like sorting emails or organizing files.

- **Pattern Recognition:** AI can quickly find patterns in data, like spotting fraud in banking or predicting the weather.

What AI Can't Do

However, AI struggles with things that require:

- **Creativity:** AI can generate text or images, but it doesn't actually "think" or come up with new ideas like a human does.

- **Emotions and Empathy:** AI can recognize words, but it doesn't truly "understand" emotions or feelings the way humans do.

- **Complex Decision-Making:** AI can analyze facts, but it doesn't have human judgment. For example, a doctor can look at a patient's symptoms, consider their emotions, and make a decision based on experience. AI, on the other hand, can only compare symptoms to a database.

At the end of the day, AI is just a tool, it's helpful, but it will always need humans to guide it.

Why Learning About AI Now Is a Good Idea (Even if You're 80!)

Some people think AI is only for young people or tech experts, but the truth is, anyone can learn about it. In fact, understanding AI now can help make life easier and more enjoyable, no matter your age.

AI Can Save You Time

Simple AI tools, like voice assistants or smart home devices, can help you with everyday tasks. You can use AI to:

- Set reminders so you never forget an important date.

- Dictate a text message instead of typing it.

- Get instant answers to questions without having to search online.

Learning how to use these tools means spending less time on small tasks and more time on things you actually enjoy.

AI Can Keep You Connected

Whether you're keeping in touch with family or learning something new, AI can help. Some ways it can keep you connected include:

- **Video Call Assistance:** AI can help improve video calls by reducing background noise and adjusting lighting.

- **Language Translation:** AI-powered apps can translate languages in real-time, making it easier to communicate with family members who speak a different language.

- **News and Updates:** AI can summarize news stories so you can stay informed without spending hours reading articles.

AI Can Make Learning Fun

It's never too late to learn something new, and AI can be a great tool for that! You can ask AI to:

- Recommend books or audiobooks based on your interests.

- Help you learn a new language by providing translations and pronunciation guides.

- Suggest new hobbies or activities based on what you like.

Instead of seeing AI as something scary, think of it as a helpful assistant that can make life more enjoyable and exciting.

Final Thoughts

AI isn't here to take over the world, it's here to help. From improving healthcare to making homes more accessible, AI is being used in ways that benefit everyone. And while AI is great at processing data and following instructions, it will never replace human creativity, emotions, and decision-making.

Most importantly, AI is not just for young people. Anyone, at any age, can learn how to use AI to make life easier and more fun. Whether it's setting reminders, translating languages, or learning something new, AI is a tool that anyone can use.

So don't be afraid of AI, embrace it! The more you understand it, the more you'll see just how helpful it can be.

CHAPTER 2: Talking to AI: How to Ask and Get What You Want

The Secret to Getting AI to Understand You

How AI Understands Language (Kind of Like a Smart Parrot)

If you've ever talked to an AI assistant like Siri, Alexa, or ChatGPT, you might have noticed that sometimes it gives you exactly what you need, and other times, it completely misunderstands you. Why does this happen? The short answer is that AI doesn't "think" the way people do, it predicts what you want based on patterns.

You might think of AI as a smart parrot. It doesn't truly understand what you're saying the way a human does, but it has learned from millions of conversations and knows how to respond in ways that seem intelligent. Let's break down exactly how AI understands (and sometimes misunderstands) human language.

AI Doesn't "Think" Like a Human, It Predicts What You Want

When you talk to another person, they understand you based on emotions, experience, and common sense. AI, on the other hand, doesn't have emotions or personal experiences. Instead, it uses something called **pattern recognition** to predict what should come next in a sentence.

Think of AI as a giant autocomplete tool. When you type a text message, your phone suggests words to finish your sentence. AI does the same thing, but on a much larger scale. It looks at the words you give it and predicts what the most likely response should be based on past conversations it has learned from.

Example:

If you ask an AI, "What's the best way to bake a cake?" it doesn't actually *know* how to bake a cake. Instead, it has seen thousands (or even millions) of similar questions and responses. It finds the most common way people answer this question and gives you a response that *sounds* correct.

Most of the time, this works well. But sometimes, AI gets things wrong because it doesn't actually "understand" the way a human does, it's just guessing based on patterns.

Why AI Sometimes Gets Things Wrong (And How to Fix That)

Because AI relies on predicting patterns, it can sometimes give weird, wrong, or even funny responses. Let's look at a few reasons why AI makes mistakes and how you can avoid them.

1. AI Can Be Too Literal

AI takes your words at face value. If you ask, "Can you tell me how to fix my Wi-Fi?" it might give you a step-by-step guide. But if you phrase it in a less direct way—like "My Wi-Fi is being annoying!", the AI might not realize you're looking for a solution.

Fix it: Be as direct as possible. Instead of saying, "I'm having trouble with my Wi-Fi," say, "Give me three steps to fix slow Wi-Fi."

2. AI Doesn't Know Context Like a Human

If you're talking to a friend, they remember what you said earlier in the conversation. AI, however, often forgets past messages unless specifically programmed to remember them.

Fix it: If you're continuing a conversation with AI, remind it of what you talked about before. Instead of saying, "What about the second option?" say, "Earlier, you mentioned two ways to fix my Wi-Fi. Can you explain the second one?"

3. AI Can't Read Between the Lines

Humans use sarcasm, jokes, and indirect language all the time. AI struggles with this. If you say, "Wow, great job, internet, for cutting out right when I needed it," a person would understand your frustration, but AI might think you're complimenting your internet!

Fix it: Use simple and clear language. Instead of sarcasm, say exactly what you mean: "My internet stopped working. Can you help me fix it?"

4. AI Might Make Up Information (Yes, Really!)

AI is trained to give you an answer, even if it's not 100% sure. Sometimes, it fills in gaps by making a guess. This is called **hallucination**, and it's one of the biggest problems with AI today.

Fix it: If you're using AI for something important, double-check its answers. If you ask AI about a medical issue or legal advice, always verify the information with a trusted source.

The Art of "Prompting" (Fancy Word for Asking AI the Right Way)

To get the best responses from AI, you need to ask questions in a way that makes it easy for the AI to understand what you want. This is called **prompting,** basically, giving the AI clear and direct instructions.

Here are a few simple tricks to make AI work better for you:

1. Be Specific

The more details you give AI, the better the answer will be.

Good prompt: "Give me three easy cake recipes that use chocolate."
Bad prompt: "Tell me about cake." (Too broad, AI doesn't know what you want.)

2. Use Step-by-Step Instructions

AI is great at following instructions when they are clear.

Good prompt: "Write me a short email to my doctor asking for an appointment next Tuesday."
Bad prompt: "Help me write an email." (AI won't know what kind of email you need.)

3. Ask for a Certain Format

If you need information in a specific way, tell the AI exactly how to format it.

Good prompt: "List five quick home remedies for a sore throat in bullet points."
Bad prompt: "Tell me how to fix a sore throat." (AI might give a long, unstructured answer.)

4. Ask AI to Think Like a Person

Sometimes, AI gives robotic answers. You can tell it to be more natural.

Good prompt: "Explain how Wi-Fi works as if you're talking to an 80-year-old."
Bad prompt: "Explain how Wi-Fi works." (AI might use too much technical jargon.)

Final Thoughts

AI is like a smart parrot, it can sound intelligent, but it doesn't actually "think" the way humans do. It predicts what to say based on past examples, which is why it sometimes gets things wrong.

The good news? You can train yourself to "talk" to AI in a way that makes it work better for you. By being specific, clear, and using step-by-step instructions, you can get AI to give you better, more useful answers.

So the next time you talk to Alexa, Google Assistant, or ChatGPT, remember: AI isn't perfect, but with the right prompts, you can make it work for you!

Writing the Perfect AI Question (Prompting 101)

If you've ever asked an AI a question and gotten a confusing or unhelpful answer, you're not alone. AI is smart, but it's not a mind reader. The way you phrase your question makes a huge difference in the quality of the response you get. That's where **prompting** comes in.

Prompting is just a fancy way of saying "asking the right way." The better your question, the better the answer AI will give you. In this guide, you'll learn how to ask AI the right way so you always get useful, clear, and accurate responses.

Be Clear, Be Direct, Be Specific

AI works best when it knows exactly what you're looking for. If your question is too broad or vague, the AI will struggle to give a helpful response. Think of it like talking to a waiter at a restaurant. If you say, "I want food," the waiter won't know what kind of food you want. But if you say, "I'd like a cheeseburger with no onions," the waiter knows exactly what to bring you.

AI is the same way. The more specific you are, the better your answer will be.

Examples:

Bad prompt: "Tell me about history."

Good prompt: "Give me 5 fun facts about the 1960s."

Why is the second one better? Because it:

- Narrows the topic to a specific time period (the 1960s).

- Asks for a certain type of information (fun facts).

- Sets a clear structure (5 facts, not a long, overwhelming answer).

The more precise your question, the better AI will understand what you need.

How to Get Better Answers by Adding Details

If you've ever received an answer that felt too simple or incomplete, it's likely because the AI didn't have enough details to go on. Adding extra details can make a huge difference.

1. Use Step-by-Step Instructions

If you need AI to help with something complex, break it down into steps.

Bad prompt: "Write an email." (Too general!)

Good prompt: "Write a polite email to my doctor requesting an appointment next Tuesday morning."

By specifying the purpose of the email, who it's for, and when the appointment is, you'll get a much more useful response.

2. Set a Tone or Style

AI can adjust its writing style if you tell it how you want something to sound.

Bad prompt: "Write me a message." (AI doesn't know the tone.)

Good prompt: "Write a friendly text message to my grandson congratulating him on his graduation."

Now, instead of a robotic-sounding message, you'll get something warm and personal.

3. Ask for a Specific Format

If you need AI to organize information a certain way, make sure to say so.

Bad prompt: "Tell me how to grow tomatoes."

Good prompt: "Give me a 5-step guide to growing tomatoes in bullet points."

By asking for bullet points and a specific number of steps, you'll get an easy-to-read response instead of a long, unstructured paragraph.

Common Prompting Mistakes (And How to Fix Them)

Even if you're clear, sometimes AI still gives odd or incorrect answers. Here are some common mistakes and how to fix them.

1. The Question is Too Open-Ended

If your question is too broad, AI doesn't know what to focus on.

Bad prompt: "Tell me about health." (Too vague, what part of health?)

Good prompt: "What are three simple exercises for seniors to improve balance and prevent falls?"

Now, AI knows exactly what type of information to give you.

2. The Question is Too Complicated

If you ask multiple things at once, AI might get confused.

Bad prompt: "What are some healthy meals, how do I cook them, and what's the best time to eat them?" (That's a lot!)

Good prompt: "Give me three healthy meal ideas with simple cooking instructions."

After getting that answer, you can then ask: "When is the best time to eat these meals for better digestion?" Breaking big questions into smaller ones leads to better responses.

3. The Question is Too Short

If you don't give enough details, AI might not provide the depth of information you need.

Bad prompt: "Tell me about exercise." (What kind of exercise? For what purpose?)

Good prompt: "What are three simple exercises for seniors to improve balance and prevent falls?"

More details lead to more useful answers.

Fun AI Prompting Tricks

Now that you know how to ask AI for information, here are some fun things you can do with prompts.

1. Make AI Write Like Someone Else

Want AI to write in a specific style? Just ask!

Good prompt: "Write a short motivational speech in the style of Winston Churchill."

2. Ask AI to Explain Something Like You're Five Years Old

If you ever get an answer that's too complicated, ask AI to simplify it.

Good prompt: "Explain quantum physics like I'm five years old."

3. Make AI Act Like a Character

AI can pretend to be anyone you want.

Good prompt: "Answer my questions as if you are a pirate from the 1700s."

Final Thoughts

Asking AI the right way is a skill that anyone can learn. By being clear, direct, and specific, you can get much better answers. Here's what to remember:

- Be specific, give AI as much detail as possible.

- Use step-by-step instructions for complex questions.

- Ask for a certain tone, style, or format.

- If you don't get a good answer, rephrase the question.

AI isn't perfect, but with the right prompts, you can make it work for you in everyday life. Whether you're asking about history, looking for recipes, or writing an email, the better your question, the better the answer you'll get.

So next time you talk to AI, take an extra second to phrase your question the right way—it could make all the difference!

Fixing AI's Mistakes: Re-Prompting Like a Pro

Have you ever asked AI a question and gotten a weird, confusing, or completely wrong answer? Maybe you asked for a simple explanation, but AI gave you a complicated, jargon-filled response. Or perhaps you requested a recipe, but the AI left out an important ingredient. When this happens, don't get frustrated, just re-prompt!

AI is smart, but it's not perfect. Sometimes, it needs a little help to give you the right answer. The good news? You can fix AI's mistakes simply by tweaking how you ask. This process is called re-prompting, which is just a fancy way of saying, "asking in a better way."

When AI Gives a Bad Answer, What Should You Do?

The first step is to figure out *why* the AI gave you a bad response. Here are the most common reasons:

1. The AI Misunderstood Your Question

AI relies on patterns and predictions, not actual understanding. If your question was vague or had multiple possible meanings, AI might have guessed wrong.

Bad AI Answer:

- You: "Tell me about Paris."

- AI: "Paris is a popular baby name."

How to Fix It:

- You: "Tell me about the city of Paris, including its history and famous landmarks."

2. The AI Gave Too Much or Too Little Information

Sometimes AI gives a response that's way too long, or too short to be helpful.

Bad AI Answer:

- You: "Explain how the internet works."

- AI: *Gives a 10-paragraph technical explanation.*

How to Fix It:

- You: "Explain how the internet works in two sentences, using simple language."

3. The AI Left Out Important Details

AI sometimes gives general answers when you need specifics.

Bad AI Answer:

- You: "Give me a spaghetti recipe."

- AI: *Lists ingredients but forgets the cooking steps.*

How to Fix It:

- You: "Give me a step-by-step guide for making spaghetti, including cooking times and temperatures."

The Power of Saying, 'Try Again, But Make It Simpler'

One of the easiest ways to fix an AI mistake is to ask it to redo its answer in a different way.

1. Simplifying Complicated Answers

If AI gives an answer that's too complex, just ask it to simplify it.

Bad AI Answer:

- You: "Explain quantum mechanics."

- AI: *Gives a long, confusing answer filled with physics jargon.*

Better Prompt:

- You: "Explain quantum mechanics in simple terms, like you're talking to a 10-year-old."

2. Shortening Long Responses

If AI gives too much information, ask it to summarize.

Bad AI Answer:

- You: "Tell me about the history of computers."

- AI: *Gives a multi-page essay.*

Better Prompt:

- You: "Summarize the history of computers in three sentences."

3. Making Answers More Fun or Interesting

Sometimes AI's response is correct but boring. You can ask it to be more engaging.

Better Prompt:

- You: "Explain how airplanes fly, but make it fun—like you're telling a bedtime story."

4. Asking AI to Provide Multiple Versions

Sometimes, you might want AI to give you a few different responses so you can choose the best one.

Better Prompt:

- You: "Rewrite this answer in three different ways: one formal, one casual, and one funny."

By having AI generate multiple versions, you can pick the one that fits your needs best.

Rewording vs. Refining, How to Get AI to Work With You

There are two main ways to fix AI's mistakes: rewording your question and refining the answer AI already gave you.

1. Rewording: Asking a Better Question

If AI completely misunderstood your question, you need to reword it.

Bad Prompt: "How do I make a cake?" (Too vague)

Better Prompt: "Give me an easy chocolate cake recipe for beginners."

Rewording helps AI understand exactly what you need.

2. Refining: Improving AI's First Answer

If AI gave a decent but not perfect answer, you can refine it instead of starting over.

How to Refine:

- "That was helpful! Now make it even shorter."

- "Can you explain that with a real-life example?"

- "Rewrite that in a friendlier tone."

- "Make this answer sound more professional."

Refining is like having a conversation with AI—you adjust as you go until you get the perfect response.

Bonus: Fun Ways to Test AI's Re-Prompting Skills

Want to practice re-prompting? Try these fun challenges:

Ask AI to Explain the Same Thing in Different Ways:

- "Explain gravity in one sentence."

- "Explain gravity like I'm five years old."

- "Explain gravity using a joke."

Challenge AI to Shorten or Expand Responses:

- "Summarize Romeo and Juliet in one sentence."

- "Now, tell me the whole story in three paragraphs."

- "Now, turn it into a funny short poem."

Make AI Answer in Different Styles:

- "Explain how to cook pasta in a serious, professional tone."

- "Explain how to cook pasta as if you were a pirate."

- "Explain how to cook pasta like a Shakespearean play."

These exercises show how re-prompting can completely change AI's responses.

Final Thoughts

AI isn't perfect, but that doesn't mean you have to settle for bad answers. If AI gives a confusing, incomplete, or overly complicated response, don't give up, just re-prompt!

Here's what to remember:

- Reword your question if AI misunderstood it.

- Ask AI to "try again, but simpler" if the answer is too complex.

- Refine AI's response by asking for a summary, examples, or a specific tone.

- Challenge AI with fun re-prompting exercises to see how much it can adapt.

By learning how to re-prompt like a pro, you can get AI to work better for you. The more you practice, the better your AI conversations will become. So next time AI gives a bad answer, don't get frustrated, just ask again, but smarter!

CHAPTER 3: Fun Ways to Use AI Right Now

How AI Can Make Life Easier and More Fun

AI as Your Personal Assistant

Imagine having a personal assistant who never gets tired, never forgets things, and is always available to help you. That's exactly what AI can be for you! Whether you need help writing an email, remembering appointments, or even figuring out how to fix your Wi-Fi, AI can step in and make life a lot easier. And the best part? You don't need to be a tech genius to use it.

Using AI to Write Emails, Reminders, and Grocery Lists

If you've ever stared at a blank screen, unsure of how to start an email, AI can save the day. It can help you write emails quickly and politely, whether you're scheduling an appointment, catching up with an old friend, or even responding to a complicated message.

How AI Can Help With Emails

Let's say you want to book an appointment with your doctor, but you're not sure how to phrase it professionally. You can ask AI:

Example Prompt:

"Write a polite email asking my doctor for an appointment next Tuesday morning."

AI will instantly generate something like this:

Subject: Appointment Request for Next Tuesday Morning

Dear Dr. Smith,

I hope you are doing well. I would like to schedule an appointment for next Tuesday morning if you have availability. Please let me know what times are open. Thank you for your time.

Best regards,
[Your Name]

With just one sentence, AI does all the work for you. If the email isn't exactly what you want, you can ask it to make changes—maybe make it sound more formal or shorter.

Reminders and To-Do Lists Made Easy

AI can also be used as a reminder service. Forgetting things is normal, but AI can help you stay organized. You can use AI-powered voice assistants like Siri, Alexa, or Google Assistant to remind you of important tasks.

Example Prompt:
"Remind me to take my medication at 8 AM every day."

Instead of trying to remember everything, AI keeps track of your schedule and reminds you exactly when you need it.

Similarly, you can use AI to create to-do lists for your day:

Example Prompt:
"Make a to-do list for my day, including exercise, grocery shopping, and calling my grandson."

AI can create a structured plan for you, helping you stay organized without stress.

AI for Grocery Lists

Have you ever gone to the grocery store and forgotten what you needed? AI can help with that, too. You can tell AI what meals you're planning, and it will generate a grocery list for you.

Example Prompt:
"I want to cook spaghetti and a salad for dinner. Make a grocery list for me."

AI will generate something like this:

- Spaghetti noodles

- Tomato sauce

- Ground beef

- Garlic

- Olive oil

- Lettuce

- Tomatoes

- Cucumbers

- Salad dressing

Now, all you have to do is check off items as you shop. No more forgotten ingredients!

Getting AI to Explain Confusing Things (Like How to Fix Your Wi-Fi)

Sometimes, technology can be frustrating. If your Wi-Fi stops working, your phone acts weird, or your TV won't turn on, AI can help you troubleshoot before you have to call customer support.

Instead of sifting through pages of complicated tech advice online, you can simply ask AI to explain things in a way that makes sense.

Example Prompt:
"My Wi-Fi isn't working. What are some simple things I can try to fix it?"

AI will likely suggest steps such as:

1. Check if your router is plugged in.

2. Restart your router by unplugging it for 30 seconds.

3. Make sure your internet bill is paid.

4. Try connecting another device to see if the issue is with your computer.

Instead of feeling overwhelmed, you now have a clear list of things to try before calling for help.

AI can also explain other confusing topics. Maybe you just got a new phone and don't understand how to change the ringtone. Instead of flipping through the manual, you can ask AI:

Example Prompt:
"How do I change the ringtone on my iPhone?"

AI will walk you through the steps in simple language, making technology much easier to manage.

Making AI Work for You: A Few More Handy Tricks

Beyond emails, reminders, and tech support, AI can help in many small ways throughout the day. Here are a few more things you might find useful:

1. AI Can Help You Plan Your Day

If you're wondering what to do with your time, AI can give you suggestions based on your schedule.

Example Prompt:
"I have a free afternoon. Suggest some fun and productive activities for me."

AI might suggest:

- Go for a walk in the park

- Try a new recipe

- Call a friend or family member

- Read a book or watch a documentary

---

2. AI Can Help You Write Letters or Messages

Want to send a thoughtful letter but don't know what to say? AI can help.

Example Prompt:
"Write a friendly letter to my granddaughter, telling her I miss her and hope she is doing well in school."

AI might generate:

Dear [Granddaughter's Name],

I hope you are doing well and having a great time in school. I miss you very much and can't wait to see you soon! I'd love to hear all about what you've been learning and any fun things you've been up to. Sending you lots of love!

Love,
Grandma

Now, all you have to do is write it down or send it as a message.

---

3. AI Can Help You Find Recipes Based on Ingredients You Have

Don't know what to cook? Just tell AI what's in your fridge, and it will suggest recipes.

Example Prompt:
"I have eggs, cheese, and bread. What can I make for breakfast?"

AI might suggest:

- Scrambled eggs with cheese on toast

- A cheese omelet

- French toast

This makes cooking much simpler and helps you use what you already have at home.

Final Thoughts

AI might seem like something only tech-savvy people can use, but in reality, it can be a simple and helpful tool for everyday life. Whether you need help writing an email, remembering an appointment, troubleshooting a tech issue, or even planning a meal, AI is like having a personal assistant in your pocket.

The best part? You don't have to be an expert to use it. Just ask AI for help in simple, clear sentences, and it will do the hard work for you.

So next time you need a reminder, a grocery list, or even a little help fixing your Wi-Fi, don't stress, just ask AI!

AI for Creativity and Entertainment

Artificial Intelligence isn't just about serious tasks like organizing schedules or helping with emails, it can also be a lot of fun! AI can tell jokes, write poems, create bedtime stories, and even help with hobbies like gardening, cooking, or learning music. Think of AI as a creative buddy that's always ready to entertain you or help you explore new interests.

Making AI Tell Jokes, Write Poems, and Create Bedtime Stories

AI has a great sense of humor (most of the time). If you need a laugh, AI can generate jokes on demand. Just ask, and it will come up with something funny, or at least something that will make you smile.

Example Prompt:
"Tell me a joke about cats."

AI might respond with:

"Why did the cat sit on the computer? Because it wanted to keep an eye on the mouse!"

Not bad, right? If you want a different kind of joke, just ask AI to try again. You can even specify what kind of joke you want, something silly, something clever, or even a pun.

AI can also write poems on any topic you choose. Want a short poem about friendship? AI can do that. Need a funny poem about coffee? No problem.

Example Prompt:
"Write me a short, funny poem about morning coffee."

AI might generate:

Morning coffee, dark and bold,
Keeps me warm when the air is cold.
One sip in, I start to wake,
Two sips in, I'm fully awake!

Not a poet yourself? No worries, AI can create poems for birthdays, holidays, or just for fun.

And if you ever need a bedtime story for grandkids, AI can craft one in seconds.

Example Prompt:
"Write a bedtime story about a brave little turtle who goes on an adventure."

AI might come up with a story about Toby the Turtle, who gets lost but finds his way home with the help of friendly fish and wise old crabs. The best part? If the story isn't quite right, you can ask AI to make it longer, simpler, or even funnier.

How AI Can Help With Hobbies

AI isn't just about words, it can also help you with your favorite hobbies! Whether you love gardening, cooking, painting, or playing music, AI can provide advice, inspiration, and step-by-step guidance.

1. Gardening Help

If you love growing plants, AI can give you tips on when to plant, how much to water, and how to keep pests away.

Example Prompt:
"Give me a 5-step guide to growing tomatoes at home."

AI might respond:

1. **Choose the Right Spot:** Pick a sunny location with at least 6 hours of sunlight per day.

2. **Use Good Soil:** Tomatoes grow best in rich, well-draining soil with compost or fertilizer.

3. **Water Regularly:** Keep the soil moist but not soggy, about an inch of water per week.

4. **Support the Plants:** Use stakes or cages to keep your tomato plants from falling over.

5. **Harvest When Ready:** Pick tomatoes when they turn red and feel slightly soft.

Instead of searching through books or guessing, you can get instant, clear answers from AI whenever you need gardening advice.

2. Cooking and Recipes

Ever wonder what to cook with the ingredients you already have? AI can suggest recipes based on what's in your fridge.

Example Prompt:
"I have chicken, rice, and broccoli. What can I make for dinner?"

AI might suggest:

- Chicken stir-fry

- Chicken and rice soup

- Grilled chicken with roasted broccoli

You can even ask AI for healthier alternatives or quicker meal ideas. If you're in the mood for baking, AI can give you simple cake recipes and even suggest ingredient substitutes.

Example Prompt:
"I want to bake cookies but don't have eggs. What can I use instead?"

AI might suggest using mashed bananas, applesauce, or yogurt as an egg substitute.

3. Learning Music or Art

If you've always wanted to learn an instrument, AI can help with that too. You can ask for simple instructions, song recommendations, or even practice exercises.

Example Prompt:
"Teach me a simple song to play on the piano."

AI might suggest:

- "Twinkle, Twinkle, Little Star"
- "Happy Birthday"
- "Mary Had a Little Lamb"

If you love painting or drawing, AI can suggest creative ideas, color combinations, or even explain different techniques.

Example Prompt:
"Give me 3 easy painting ideas for beginners."

AI might suggest:

1. **Sunset Over the Ocean:** Use simple brushstrokes to blend warm colors.

2. **A Field of Flowers:** Start with a green background and dot different colors for flowers.

3. **A Silhouette of a Tree:** Paint a colorful sky and add a black tree outline in the front.

Whether it's art, music, or photography, AI can give you step-by-step instructions and inspiration.

Bonus: Fun AI Games and Challenges

Want to have even more fun with AI? Try these creative challenges:

Ask AI to create a funny story using three random words.
Example Prompt: *"Write a short story using the words 'penguin,' 'balloon,' and 'banana'."*

Play "Finish the Story" with AI. Start a sentence and ask AI to continue.
Example Prompt: *"Once upon a time, a cat found a magic key..."*

Have AI generate a tongue-twister for you.
Example Prompt: *"Make up a new tongue-twister about a squirrel."*

AI can be a great source of creativity, entertainment, and learning, making everyday moments a little more exciting.

Final Thoughts

AI isn't just about work, it can be fun, too! Whether you want a joke, a poem, or a bedtime story, AI can create something unique for you in seconds. It can also help you with hobbies, from gardening and cooking to learning music or painting.

The best part? AI never runs out of ideas. If you ever feel stuck or uninspired, just ask AI for a little creativity boost. You never know what fun or fascinating response you'll get next!

So go ahead, have fun, be creative, and let AI bring a little extra joy to your day!

AI for Staying Informed and Connected

In today's fast-paced world, staying informed and keeping in touch with loved ones can sometimes feel overwhelming. But AI is here to help. Whether you want to catch up on the latest news without all the drama, communicate with family members across the world, or translate a foreign phrase in seconds, AI can make these tasks easier and more enjoyable. You don't need to be tech-savvy to use it, all you need to know is how to ask.

Using AI to Get News Summaries (Without the Drama)

Watching the news on TV or scrolling through articles online can sometimes be exhausting. There's so much information out there, and let's be honest, not all of it is reliable. Sometimes, news channels add too much drama or focus on negative stories, making it stressful to stay informed.

This is where AI comes in. AI can summarize news stories for you in a calm, straightforward way. You can ask AI to give you a quick update on what's happening in the world, and it will pull information from trusted sources, removing unnecessary exaggeration.

Example Prompt:
"Give me a simple summary of today's top news stories."

AI might respond:

- **Weather:** A heatwave is expected in some parts of the country this week.

- **Politics:** The government is discussing a new healthcare policy.

- **Sports:** The local baseball team won its game last night.

- **Entertainment:** A famous singer just announced a new album release.

You can even ask AI to summarize specific types of news:

Example Prompt:
"Summarize today's health news in two sentences."

AI might respond:

- "Scientists have developed a new treatment for arthritis that shows promising results. Doctors also recommend more vitamin D for better bone health."

This way, you get just the facts, no unnecessary drama, no overwhelming details, just the information you need to stay updated.

Translating Languages (Talk to Family Across the World)

Do you have family members or friends who speak another language? Maybe you want to send a message to a relative overseas, or you're traveling and need to understand a street sign. AI can translate words and phrases instantly, making communication easier than ever.

Instead of flipping through a dictionary or guessing what something means, just ask AI.

Example Prompt:
"Translate 'How are you?' into five different languages."

AI might respond:

- Spanish: **¿Cómo estás?**

- French: **Comment ça va?**

- German: **Wie geht es dir?**

- Italian: **Come stai?**

- Japanese: **元気ですか？(Genki desu ka?)**

If you need to write a longer message, AI can translate full sentences while keeping them natural.

Example Prompt:
"Translate this sentence into Spanish: 'Hi Grandma, I hope you're having a wonderful day!'"

AI might respond:

- **Hola Abuela, espero que estés teniendo un día maravilloso.**

This can be incredibly helpful when sending holiday greetings, birthday wishes, or just keeping in touch with family members who speak a different language.

And if you're traveling, AI can help you read menus, signs, or even understand spoken language in real time with translation apps.

Example Prompt:
"How do I say 'Where is the nearest bathroom?' in French?"

AI will give you the translation so you can confidently ask for help wherever you are.

Using AI to Stay Connected Through Social Media and Messaging

AI can also help you stay in touch with friends and family by assisting with social media, emails, and messages.

1. Helping You Write Better Messages

If you ever struggle with how to phrase something, AI can suggest the best way to say it.

Example Prompt:
"Write a short, friendly message to my cousin asking how they've been."

AI might generate:

"Hey [Cousin's Name], I was just thinking about you! How have you been? Hope everything is going well. Let's catch up soon!"

2. Making It Easier to Post on Social Media

If you like sharing updates on Facebook or Instagram but don't know what to write, AI can help.

Example Prompt:
"Write a short and cheerful Facebook post about how much I love my morning coffee."

AI might suggest:

"Nothing beats the smell of fresh coffee in the morning! Starting the day with my favorite cup and a big smile. Hope you all have a great day!"

Even if you don't use social media much, AI can help you write comments, captions, or even find the right words to wish someone a happy birthday.

Example Prompt:

"Write a sweet birthday message for my friend Mary."

AI might generate:

"Happy Birthday, Mary! I hope you have a fantastic day filled with laughter, love, and all your favorite things. Wishing you a wonderful year ahead!"

AI for Quick and Easy Answers

Ever been curious about something but didn't want to search through endless websites to find an answer? AI can act as your personal information assistant, providing answers quickly and clearly.

1. Understanding Technology

If you're struggling with a tech issue, AI can give step-by-step instructions.

Example Prompt:

"How do I reset my Wi-Fi router?"

AI might respond:

1. Unplug your router from the power outlet.

2. Wait for 30 seconds.

3. Plug it back in and wait for the lights to turn on.

4. Try reconnecting your device to the internet.

No need to call customer support, AI can walk you through it!

2. Quick Facts and Trivia

Want to impress your grandkids with fun facts? AI can give you trivia on any topic.

Example Prompt:
"Tell me a fun fact about elephants."

AI might respond:

- "Did you know that elephants use their trunks like a straw to drink water, but they never actually drink through their trunks? They use them to suck up water and pour it into their mouths!"

Final Thoughts

AI is an incredible tool for staying informed and connected. Whether you want to keep up with the news without the stress, translate messages to loved ones, or simply stay in touch through social media and messaging, AI makes everything easier.

With just a simple question, you can get news summaries, learn how to fix a tech problem, translate languages, and even find fun facts to share with friends and family.

No matter your age or experience with technology, AI is here to help you stay connected with the world. So go ahead, ask AI anything, and let it do the hard work for you!

CHAPTER 4: AI Tools You Can Try Today (For Free!)

The Easiest AI Apps for Beginners

Chatbots: Talking to AI in a Chat Window

One of the easiest ways to experience AI for yourself is by using a chatbot. A chatbot is simply a program that you can talk to in a chat window, just like texting a friend. Instead of texting a human, though, you're chatting with an AI that can answer questions, give advice, tell jokes, and even help you write things.

If you've ever used a virtual assistant like Siri or Alexa, then you're already familiar with the concept of talking to AI. But AI chatbots take it a step further, they can have full conversations, help with planning, and even provide creative ideas. The best part? Many of these chatbots are completely free to use!

Popular Free AI Chatbots You Can Try Today

There are several AI chatbots available online, and they all have different strengths. Let's take a look at some of the most popular ones and what they're best for.

1. ChatGPT (by OpenAI)

Best for: General conversations, creative writing, explanations, and brainstorming ideas.

ChatGPT is one of the most well-known AI chatbots. It's designed to sound natural, making it feel like you're having a conversation with a real person. You can ask it questions, request help with writing, or just chat for fun.

Example Uses:

- **Ask for a summary:** "Can you explain World War II in simple terms?"

- **Get creative ideas:** "Give me three ideas for a birthday gift for my grandson."

- **Help with writing:** "Write me a short thank-you note for my neighbor."

It's also great for learning new things! You can ask ChatGPT for quick explanations on anything from history to science to technology.

Example Prompt:
"Tell me 3 fun facts about Paris in a simple way."

AI might respond:

1. **Paris has a hidden city underneath it!** There are miles of underground tunnels called the Catacombs, filled with old bones from millions of people.

2. **The Eiffel Tower changes size!** Because of temperature changes, the metal expands and shrinks, making the tower a little taller in summer.

3. **Paris has a rule about building heights!** Unlike other big cities, you won't see too many tall skyscrapers in the center of Paris to keep its historic look.

ChatGPT is easy to use, just type your question, and it responds instantly.

---

2. Google Bard

Best for: Fact-checking, finding up-to-date information, and answering tricky questions.

Google Bard is Google's AI chatbot, designed to help with research and quick answers. Unlike ChatGPT, which doesn't always have the latest news, Bard is connected to the internet and can give you the most current information available.

Example Uses:

- **Get real-time news updates:** "What's the latest weather forecast for New York?"

- **Fact-check something:** "Is it true that coffee helps you live longer?"

- **Learn about current events:** "Tell me about the latest space exploration news."

If you ever want to confirm whether something is true, Bard is a good AI chatbot to ask because it pulls from live sources.

---

3. Microsoft Copilot (Formerly Bing Chat)

Best for: Searching the web, answering questions, and summarizing information.

Microsoft Copilot (also known as Bing Chat) works a lot like Google Bard, but it also gives direct links to where it found its answers. This makes it great for looking up facts, finding reliable sources, and even shopping for products.

Example Uses:

- **Look up travel tips:** "What are the best places to visit in Italy?"

- **Compare products:** "What's the difference between an iPhone 13 and an iPhone 14?"

- **Find cooking tips:** "How do I make a fluffy pancake?"

Copilot is helpful if you need to do a quick internet search but don't want to scroll through multiple websites. It gathers information for you in seconds.

---

4. Pi (Personal AI Assistant)

Best for: Casual conversation, emotional support, and friendly chats.

Pi is a different kind of AI chatbot, it's designed to be a supportive, friendly companion. While other chatbots focus on answering questions, Pi is meant for casual conversation. It's great if you just want to chat, share your thoughts, or even get some encouragement.

Example Uses:

- **Daily check-ins:** "Ask me how my day is going."

- **Friendly motivation:** "Give me a little pep talk before my doctor's appointment."

- **Lighthearted fun:** "Tell me a funny story about a cat."

Pi is less about finding information and more about making you feel heard and supported.

How to Use AI Chatbots Effectively

Now that you know about different chatbots, how do you actually get the best responses from them? Here are some simple tips:

1. Be Clear and Specific

AI chatbots work best when you ask clear and specific questions.

Not Specific Enough: "Tell me about history."
Better Question: "Give me 5 fun facts about the 1960s."

The more details you include, the better the response will be.

---

2. Ask for Summaries or Simple Explanations

If AI gives you a long or complicated answer, you can ask it to summarize or simplify.

Example Prompt:
"Explain photosynthesis in two sentences using simple words."

AI might respond:

"Plants use sunlight, water, and air to make their own food. This process is called photosynthesis, and it helps them grow."

3. Ask AI to Personalize Responses

You can ask AI to tailor its answers to fit your needs.

Example Prompt:
"Give me an easy 10-minute exercise routine for seniors."

AI might suggest:

1. Stretch your arms and legs for 2 minutes.

2. March in place for 3 minutes.

3. Do light chair squats for 2 minutes.

4. Stretch your neck and shoulders for 3 minutes.

This makes AI responses more practical and useful for your lifestyle.

Final Thoughts

Chatbots are an easy and fun way to experience AI. Whether you need help finding information, want a quick laugh, or just want someone (or something!) to chat with, AI chatbots can do it all. The best part? You don't need any technical skills, just type your question and let AI do the rest.

If you've never tried talking to an AI chatbot before, start with ChatGPT, Google Bard, or Microsoft Copilot. They are free, easy to use, and can help with everything from writing messages to finding fun facts.

So why not give it a try? Ask a chatbot something fun, like:

Example Prompt:

"Tell me a fun fact about penguins!"

Who knows? You might just discover your new favorite digital assistant!

AI That Listens: Voice Assistants Like Siri & Alexa

Imagine having a personal assistant who never sleeps, never forgets, and is always ready to help at a moment's notice. That's exactly what voice assistants like **Siri, Alexa, and Google Assistant** are designed to do. These AI-powered helpers listen to your voice commands and respond instantly, making everyday tasks easier and more convenient. Whether you want to set a reminder, check the weather, or even play your favorite song, all you have to do is ask.

Voice assistants have become a part of many households, and for a good reason—they make life simpler. But what exactly can they do? And just as importantly, what **can't** they do? Let's dive into the world of voice assistants and explore how they can make your daily routine smoother.

What Voice Assistants Can Do (And What They Can't)

Voice assistants are designed to **listen, process, and respond** to your voice commands. Their abilities vary depending on which assistant you use and the device it's connected to. Here are some of the most common things they can do:

What They Can Do:

Answer Quick Questions: Ask about the weather, news, or trivia facts.

Set Reminders and Alarms: Never forget an appointment or medication again.

Control Smart Home Devices: Adjust the lights, thermostat, or TV (if connected).

Play Music or Podcasts: Ask for your favorite songs or radio stations.

Make Calls or Send Messages: Use voice commands to contact friends or family.

Provide Directions: Get step-by-step guidance while driving.

Tell Jokes and Fun Facts: Just for entertainment!

Example Prompt:
"Alexa, what's the weather like today?"

AI might respond:

"Today in New York, it's sunny with a high of 75°F and a low of 60°F."

However, while voice assistants are very helpful, they do have limitations.

What They Can't Do:

Have Deep Conversations: Unlike chatbots like ChatGPT, voice assistants are better at short, direct commands rather than long conversations.

Make Complex Decisions: They can suggest things, but they can't think like a human.

Understand Everything Perfectly: Sometimes, they mishear or misinterpret what you say.

Work Without an Internet Connection: Most voice assistants need Wi-Fi to function.

Knowing what voice assistants can and can't do will help you use them effectively and avoid frustration.

Using Voice Assistants for Reminders, Alarms, and Quick Questions

One of the best ways to use a voice assistant is to **set reminders, alarms, and ask quick questions,** all without lifting a finger.

1. Setting Reminders

If you often forget small tasks, voice assistants can help you remember.

Example Prompt:
"Siri, remind me to take my medicine at 8 AM every day."

AI will confirm and then notify you at the correct time each day.

Other Example Prompts:

- "Alexa, remind me to call my daughter at 3 PM."

- "Google, remind me to water my plants every Friday."

Reminders can be one-time or recurring, making them great for things like **paying bills, birthdays, and appointments.**

---

2. Setting Alarms and Timers

If you need to wake up at a specific time or set a timer while cooking, your voice assistant can handle it.

Example Prompt:
"Alexa, set an alarm for 7 AM tomorrow."

AI will set the alarm and wake you up at the correct time.

Other Example Prompts:

- "Siri, set a timer for 20 minutes." (Perfect for baking or workouts.)

- "Google, wake me up at 6 AM on weekdays."

Setting alarms and timers with just your voice is **quick, easy, and hands-free.**

---

3. Asking Quick Questions

Voice assistants are great for answering simple questions without needing to type anything.

Example Prompt:
"Google, how far is Los Angeles from New York?"

AI might respond:

"The distance between Los Angeles and New York is about 2,800 miles."

Other Example Prompts:

- "Alexa, how many cups are in a quart?" (Helpful for cooking!)

- "Siri, who won the last Super Bowl?"

- "Google, translate 'Good morning' into French."

For **basic facts, measurements, and translations,** voice assistants are incredibly useful.

Using Voice Assistants for Fun and Entertainment

Besides helping with practical tasks, voice assistants can also be used for **entertainment, relaxation, and even learning new things.**

1. Playing Music and Podcasts

If you enjoy listening to music, audiobooks, or podcasts, just ask AI to play them for you.

Example Prompt:
"Alexa, play relaxing jazz music."

AI will find a jazz playlist and start playing it instantly.

Other Example Prompts:

- "Siri, play my '80s music playlist."

- "Google, play a podcast about history."

If you have a **smart speaker**, AI can fill the room with your favorite tunes, making it **perfect for background music while cooking or relaxing.**

---

2. Telling Jokes and Fun Facts

Need a laugh? Ask your voice assistant to tell you a joke!

Example Prompt:

"Alexa, tell me a joke."

AI might respond:

"Why did the scarecrow win an award? Because he was outstanding in his field!"

Other Example Prompts:

- "Siri, give me a fun fact about space."

- "Google, tell me a bedtime story."

You can also ask voice assistants to play games, do trivia quizzes, or even tell **riddles and tongue twisters.**

Making Calls and Sending Messages with AI

Some voice assistants, like Siri and Alexa, can help you **call or message people hands-free.**

Example Prompt:

"Siri, call my daughter."

AI will dial the number for you. This is **especially useful if your hands are busy or you have mobility issues.**

Other Example Prompts:

- "Alexa, send a text to John saying 'I'll be there in 10 minutes.'"

- "Google, call the nearest pharmacy."

This feature makes it easy to **stay connected with family and friends** without having to manually dial numbers.

Final Thoughts

Voice assistants like Siri, Alexa, and Google Assistant are **incredibly helpful** for everyday tasks. They can:
Set reminders so you never forget important things.
Answer questions instantly.
Play music, podcasts, or audiobooks.
Tell jokes, fun facts, or bedtime stories.
Make calls and send messages.

They aren't perfect, and they can sometimes misunderstand what you say. But once you get used to how they work, they can be a **great companion** for making life easier and more enjoyable.

If you've never used a voice assistant before, try starting with something simple like:

Example Prompt:
"Alexa, what's the weather like today?"

Who knows? You might find yourself relying on AI more than you ever expected!

AI for Writing, Pictures, and Even Music

AI isn't just for answering questions or setting reminders, it can also help spark creativity! Whether you need to **write an email, summarize a long article, create a bedtime story, turn words into pictures, or even generate music**, AI can assist in ways that make the creative process easier and more fun. The best part? You don't need to be a professional writer, artist, or musician to use these tools. With just a simple request, AI can help bring your ideas to life.

AI for Writing Emails, Summaries, and Creative Stories

Writing can sometimes feel like a chore, especially when you're trying to phrase something just right. AI can take the pressure off by helping you write **emails, letters, summaries, and even full stories** with just a few simple instructions.

1. AI for Writing Emails

Have you ever sat in front of your computer or phone, unsure of how to start an email? Whether you're making an appointment, responding to a friend, or sending a thank-you note, AI can help craft the perfect message in seconds.

Example Prompt:
"Write a polite email to my doctor asking for an appointment next Wednesday at 10 AM."

AI might generate:

Subject: Appointment Request for Wednesday at 10 AM

Dear Dr. Smith,

I hope you are doing well. I would like to schedule an appointment for next Wednesday at 10 AM if you have availability. Please let me know if that time works or if another slot is open. Thank you for your time.

Best regards,
[Your Name]

You can even ask AI to make the email **more formal, shorter, or friendlier**, depending on what you need.

2. AI for Summarizing Long Texts

If you've ever come across a long article or book passage and wanted a quick summary, AI can do that for you in seconds. Instead of reading through pages of information, AI can **condense** it into key points.

Example Prompt:
"Summarize this article about healthy eating in two sentences."

AI might respond:

"Eating a balanced diet with plenty of fruits, vegetables, and whole grains can help improve overall health. Avoiding processed foods and sugary drinks is key to maintaining good nutrition."

If you need **more detail**, you can ask AI to summarize in a **paragraph instead of two sentences.**

3. AI for Writing Fun Stories

Sometimes, you just want to let your imagination run wild. AI can **help create stories** based on your ideas, whether it's a bedtime story for your grandkids or just something fun for yourself.

Example Prompt:
"Make a short bedtime story about a cat who can fly."

AI might generate:

Once upon a time, there was a little cat named Whiskers who dreamed of flying. One night, under the light of a full moon,

Whiskers found a pair of magical wings in the backyard. He flapped them and soared into the sky!

Whiskers flew over houses, trees, and even the ocean, making friends with the birds along the way. But when he saw his owner looking sad, missing him, he knew it was time to return home. Whiskers landed gently on his bed, happy to be back but excited for his next adventure in the sky.

You can ask AI to make the story **longer, shorter, funnier, or even written as a poem.**

AI Art Tools: Turning Words into Pictures

Another exciting use of AI is **creating pictures from words.** You can describe an image, and AI will generate it for you. This is useful for **fun projects, digital art, or just exploring creativity.**

1. How AI Art Works

Instead of painting with a brush or sketching with a pencil, AI "draws" by analyzing thousands of existing images and combining elements to create something new. You simply tell the AI what you want, and it generates an image in seconds.

Example Prompt:
"Create a painting of a cat wearing sunglasses and playing the guitar."

AI might generate a **fun, colorful image** of a cool cat rocking out on a stage.

2. Is AI Art Really "Art"?

Some people wonder if AI-generated images count as real art. After all, a computer is creating the picture, not a human. But many artists use AI as a tool to enhance their work, just like photographers use cameras or painters use brushes. AI can help bring ideas to life, but it still needs a human to **guide it with a creative vision.**

For beginners, AI art is a **fun and easy way** to experiment with creating pictures **without needing drawing skills.**

Other Fun AI Art Prompts:

- "Make a drawing of a castle in the clouds."

- "Create a realistic painting of a golden retriever sitting in a flower field."

- "Turn my selfie into a painting in the style of Van Gogh."

These tools make it possible for anyone to create unique images, whether for fun or professional use.

AI for Music: Composing Without an Instrument

AI can also **help create music,** even if you don't play an instrument! Whether you want a relaxing melody, a fun tune for a video, or just background music while working, AI-powered music tools can generate original compositions in seconds.

1. How AI Music Works

AI listens to thousands of songs and learns patterns in melodies, rhythms, and harmonies. When you give it instructions, it creates a **new song from scratch** based on what it has learned.

Example Prompt:

"Create a calm piano melody for relaxation."

AI will generate a gentle, soothing piano piece that can be used for meditation, studying, or falling asleep.

---

2. Different Ways to Use AI Music

You can ask AI to generate songs in different styles, including jazz, pop, or classical.

Other Fun AI Music Prompts:

- "Make a happy ukulele tune for a summer picnic."
- "Create an exciting drumbeat for an action movie scene."
- "Generate a peaceful nature soundscape with soft rain and birds singing."

Whether you're a musician or just love listening to music, AI makes it easy to explore new sounds and styles.

Final Thoughts

AI isn't just for answering questions, it can be a **powerful creative tool** that helps with **writing, art, and music.**

Need to write an email? AI can help you phrase it perfectly.
Want to summarize a long article? AI can give you the key points in seconds.
Looking for a fun bedtime story? AI can create one on the spot.
Interested in digital art? AI can turn your words into pictures.
Curious about music? AI can compose a melody based on your request.

The best part? You don't have to be an expert in writing, drawing, or music to **have fun and be creative** with AI. Just describe what you want, and AI will bring your ideas to life.

So go ahead, try it out! You might be surprised at what AI can create for you.

CHAPTER 5: Final Thoughts + Let's Practice!

Let's Put Your AI Knowledge to the Test

AI Is Not Magic, It's Just Another Tool

Artificial Intelligence might seem like something out of a science fiction movie, but it's not magic. It's simply a tool, one that can make life easier in many ways but still has limits. Just like a calculator helps with math or a microwave heats up food, AI is a tool designed to **assist, not replace human thinking.**

Understanding AI as a **useful tool rather than a magical machine** will help you use it wisely. AI can do a lot, from answering questions to creating stories and images, but it's not perfect. It doesn't "think" the way humans do, and sometimes, it even makes mistakes. That's why knowing how to use it correctly, and when to **double-check its answers,** is just as important as learning how to use it at all.

AI Is Great, But It's Not Perfect

AI is **fast, smart, and helpful**, but it's not always right. Because AI is trained by analyzing patterns in text, images, and data, it sometimes makes **wrong guesses** or presents **incorrect facts.**

Think about it like this: AI is like a student who has read a lot of books but never actually experienced the real world. It can give great answers based on what it has learned, but if it comes across something it doesn't fully understand, it might **guess incorrectly** instead of admitting it doesn't know.

For example, let's say you ask AI:

Example Prompt:
"Who was the 50th President of the United States?"

AI might respond with **a completely made-up name.** Why? Because the U.S. hasn't had a 50th president yet! But instead of saying, **"There is no 50th president,"** AI might try to **guess** based on patterns in previous questions.

That's why AI is a great **assistant** but not a perfect **teacher.** It can help explain things, generate ideas, and make tasks easier, but it's always a good idea to **verify important information.**

The Importance of Checking Information (AI Sometimes Lies!)

Just because AI gives you an answer **doesn't mean it's correct.** Sometimes, AI makes mistakes by accident, and other times, it fills in gaps with **completely false information** (this is called "hallucination" in AI terms).

Here's why you should **always double-check AI's answers:**

1. AI Can Make Up Facts

AI doesn't "know" facts like a person does. It just predicts what words should come next based on patterns. If there isn't a clear answer, it might **invent one** rather than leave the question unanswered.

Example Prompt:
"Who invented the internet?"

AI might say:

"The internet was invented by John Smith in 1965."

Sounds official, right? **But it's false.** The internet was developed by multiple people, including Vinton Cerf and Robert Kahn, over several years. AI **might not always give credit to the right people.**

How to Check:

- Google the same question and compare results from trusted sources.

- Ask AI: **"Can you show me your sources for this answer?"**

---

2. AI Can Get Dates and Numbers Wrong

AI is trained on information available **at the time of its last update.** If you ask it about a recent event, it might not have the latest details.

Example Prompt:
"Who won the last Olympic Games?"

If AI hasn't been updated recently, it might **list the wrong country or year.**

How to Check:

- Use **news websites** for up-to-date events.

- Ask AI to **cite a source** or provide links.

3. AI Might Not Understand Context

Sometimes, AI takes things **too literally** or **misunderstands what you mean.**

Example Prompt:
"How many stars are in the sky?"

AI might **try to guess a number** (like "100 trillion stars") instead of saying:

"The exact number of stars in the universe is unknown."

How to Check:

- Reword the question to be **more specific.**

- Ask for **multiple sources** of information.

How to Keep Practicing and Learning More

The best way to get better at using AI is to **keep experimenting!** The more you practice, the better you'll understand how to ask questions and get useful answers. Here's how to **continue improving your AI skills:**

1. Ask AI Different Types of Questions

Try asking AI about different topics to see how it responds.

Fun Example Prompts:

- "Tell me a joke about dogs."

- "Explain gravity like I'm five years old."

- "Give me 3 tips for staying organized at home."

By testing AI with different topics, you'll learn how it **responds best.**

---

2. Compare AI's Answers to Other Sources

Anytime AI gives you a **fact-based answer**, compare it with other sources to make sure it's correct.

Example Prompt:
"What are the benefits of drinking green tea?"

How to verify:

- Check **health websites** or articles written by **experts.**

- Look for **recent studies** rather than just one answer from AI.

Practicing this habit **prevents misinformation** and ensures you get the **best knowledge.**

---

3. Use AI to Help You Learn New Skills

AI can be a **great learning tool** when used correctly. If you're interested in a **new hobby, skill, or language**, AI can guide you step by step.

Example Learning Prompts:

- "Teach me 5 basic words in Spanish."

- "Give me an easy recipe for homemade bread."

- "What's a good way to start learning photography?"

AI can **offer tips, guides, and explanations,** but remember to **cross-check advice with reliable sources.**

4. Practice Refining Your Prompts

AI works best when you **ask clearly and specifically.** If an answer isn't helpful, **rephrase the question!**

Example of Improving a Question:
Not specific enough: "Tell me about history."
Better question: "Give me 5 interesting facts about the 1960s."

By adjusting how you ask, you'll get **better responses.**

Final Thoughts

AI is a powerful tool, but **it's not perfect,** and that's okay! It's meant to be a **helpful assistant**, not a **replacement for thinking and learning.**

Here's what to remember:
AI can help you find answers, but always **double-check important information.**
AI doesn't "know" things, it **predicts** based on past information, which means it can make mistakes.
Keep **practicing and experimenting** to get better at using AI for everyday tasks.

The more you use AI, the more comfortable you'll get. Whether it's for **fun, learning, or everyday convenience,** AI can be an **amazing tool** when used wisely.

So go ahead, **ask AI something new today, and see what happens!**

The Right and Wrong Ways to Use AI

Artificial Intelligence is an incredible tool, but like any tool, it needs to be used **the right way.** AI can help with many things, writing, organizing, learning, and even entertainment, but it has limits. It's important to **understand what AI can and can't do,** when to use it, and how to use it responsibly.

Some people think AI can replace real people, but that's not true. Others worry about privacy and whether AI is "watching" them. And then there's the question of **how to use AI in a way that helps, rather than harms.** Let's take a closer look at **the right and wrong ways to use AI** so you can make the most of it without running into problems.

AI Is Not a Replacement for Real People

AI is **smart, but not human.** It can **answer questions, write stories, and generate ideas**, but it doesn't have emotions, personal experiences, or real judgment. Some people treat AI like a human, but at the end of the day, AI is **just a machine that predicts words and patterns.**

AI Can Help, But It Can't Think for You

AI is great at **providing suggestions, summaries, and explanations.** However, **it doesn't actually "think" or "understand" things the way humans do.**

AI processes **patterns** in information, it doesn't have thoughts, feelings, or opinions of its own. It doesn't understand **context** like a human does. If you ask it for advice, it can give you suggestions based on common responses, but it doesn't actually "know" the best decision for you.

For example, if you ask AI **which city is better to live in**, it might list the pros and cons, but it **doesn't know your personal preferences,** like whether you prefer warm weather or cold winters.

Example: If you ask AI to write a letter for you, it can create a **polite and well-structured message.** But if the letter needs **emotional depth or personal details**, only you can provide that.

Example Prompt:
"Write a thank-you letter to my friend for helping me move."

AI might generate something like this:

Dear [Friend's Name],

Thank you so much for helping me move last weekend. I truly appreciate your time and effort, it made a big difference. I couldn't have done it without you! Let's get together soon so I can treat you to a meal as a thank-you.

Best,
[Your Name]

This is a **great starting point,** but **only you** can add personal details like:

- **A specific memory** ("I'll never forget how you managed to fit that giant couch through the tiny doorway!")

- **A shared joke** ("I owe you one, next time, I promise I won't make you carry all the heavy boxes!")

So while AI can assist, **it shouldn't replace personal effort in human relationships.**

AI Can't Replace Human Connections

Some people rely on AI for conversation or companionship, which is fine in moderation. But AI **shouldn't replace real human relationships.**

Example:
Some AI chatbots are designed to provide conversation, and while they can be fun, they **can't truly understand emotions** the way real friends and family can.

Instead of replacing real human interactions, use AI as a tool to:
Find new conversation starters.
Practice social skills.
Get advice (but always think critically about AI's suggestions).

The best connections still come from **real conversations** with family, friends, and loved ones.

Privacy: What AI Can See and What It Can't

Some people worry that AI **is always listening or watching,** but in reality, most AI chatbots **do not** have access to private information unless you give it to them. However, it's still **important to be cautious** with what you share.

AI Chatbots Can't See Your Private Data

Most AI systems **don't automatically know who you are, where you live, or what's on your phone.**

Example: If you ask AI, **"What's my address?"** it won't know unless you've **told it** in a previous conversation.

What AI Can See:

- The words you type or speak during the conversation.

- General knowledge available online (depending on the AI).

What AI Can't See:

- Your personal messages, emails, or photos.

- Your bank details or passwords.

- Your private conversations outside of the chat window.

That said, if you type **personal details into AI**, they may be stored on the system. **Always be careful about what you share!**

Best Practice: Never give AI sensitive information, like your Social Security number, bank details, or personal secrets.

Be Aware of AI Listening Devices (Like Siri & Alexa)

Devices like **Siri, Alexa, and Google Assistant do listen for their wake words** ("Hey Siri" or "Alexa"), but they **aren't always recording everything you say.**

How to Protect Your Privacy:
Check your settings, many devices **allow you to delete voice recordings.**
Mute your voice assistant when not in use.
Be careful what personal details you say out loud when AI devices are active.

While AI is designed to **help, not spy**, it's always good to take precautions to **protect your privacy.**

How to Use AI Responsibly

AI is a powerful tool, but **like any tool, it should be used wisely.** Here are some simple **do's and don'ts** to make sure you're using AI in a helpful and ethical way.

DO: Use AI to Learn and Grow

AI is **great for learning**, whether you want to pick up a new skill, get quick explanations, or even practice a new language.

Example Prompts:

- "Teach me 5 words in Italian."

- "Give me a simple explanation of how the stock market works."

- "Help me create a daily exercise routine."

Using AI for **education and self-improvement** is a **responsible and beneficial** way to use this technology.

DON'T: Use AI to Cheat or Spread False Information

Some people use AI to **cheat on tests, copy answers, or spread misinformation.** This is an **irresponsible** use of AI.

Example:
If a student uses AI to write an entire essay **without reading it** or adding their own thoughts, they **aren't actually learning.**

Better Way: Use AI for guidance, but **write in your own words.**

DO: Double-Check AI's Answers

AI **isn't always right.** Before using AI-generated information, **check reliable sources.**

Example Prompt:
"What are the symptoms of high blood pressure?"

Instead of trusting AI **without verification**, check **health websites or talk to a doctor.**

Final Thoughts

AI is a fantastic tool, but it's **not a replacement for real people.** It's important to:
Use AI for learning, creativity, and assistance.
Be mindful of privacy and never share sensitive details.
Double-check information before believing or sharing it.
Use AI responsibly and ethically.

When used the right way, AI can **make life easier and more interesting.** But just like any tool, it's up to **you** to use it wisely.

So go ahead, explore AI, have fun, and **use it in ways that help, not harm!**

Final Exercises: Let's Try AI Together!	

Exercise 1: Talking to AI for Help
- Use a chatbot like ChatGPT. Ask it:
  - 'What are 3 easy dinner recipes with chicken?'
  - 'Summarize today's news in simple words.'
- Compare how different AI tools respond!
	Exercise 2: Making AI Work for You
	- Ask AI to help with something practical in your life:
	  - Example: 'Write a polite text message asking my neighbor to water my plants.'
	- Try re-prompting: If the first answer isn't great, adjust your question and try again.

Answer: (Write AI's response here)	

Final Words: You Did It! Now What?

• You've taken your first steps into AI, now it's time to use what you've learned.

- Stay curious, keep experimenting, and don't be afraid to ask AI anything.

- **Get ready for Book 2 in the series, where we'll explore even more AI tools you can start using today!**

www.ingramcontent.com/pod-product-compliance
Lightning Source LLC
LaVergne TN
LVHW051536050326
832903LV00033B/4266